Future Choice

Why Network Marketing may be
your BEST career move

Michael S. Clouse
Kathie Jackson Anderson

D0168395

Candlelight Press
Seattle 1993

ISBN: 0-9635949-0-7
Library of Congress Catalog Card Number: 93-070272

Future

Choice

———

TABLE

OF

CONTENTS

———

)

I HEARTILY RECOMMEND THIS APTLY TITLED and well-written book to anyone seeking to learn about opportunities in network marketing.

I personally learned about the power of network marketing somewhat reluctantly. Like so many people, my mind was mainly closed on the subject. Then one of my editors at SUCCESS began urging me to let him do a report for our readers on the topic. I explained to the staffer that, based on what little I knew, I had a hard time believing that network marketing could be seen as a serious way of building a business or making a living. "Some of the stories are simply too good to be true," I said, attempting to close the matter.

As it happened, I was dealing with Senior Editor Richard Poe, who had spent months examining the issue and preparing arguments to present to me and my other editors. In our ensuing editorial meetings, as Poe recounted statistics, case studies and anecdotes, I found myself becoming more receptive to his proposal.

However, some staffers considered the entire subject one to be shunned. As the opposing editors sensed my interest in the topic growing, they called a "time out" so they could gather material to present the opposite point of view. With the help of our researchers and our Nexus on-line service, our offices were soon flooded with network marketing articles from the national press. I read stacks of them, noting how public officials and regulators frequently made critical comments about network marketing or multi-level marketing, as it is often called.

But what all the previous coverage demonstrated to me was different that what my staff critics had intended. What the articles made clear was that the other side of the story -- the positive side -- had never been told. Why was this the case? Because the press in general, and the business press in particular, is, by and large, not opportunity-oriented. The journalistic mindset is inclined to be skeptical, critical, doubting, analytical -- all important traits, to be sure. But what was needed to see the network marketing story was a receptive, entrepreneurial, future-oriented perspective -- a mindset that seeks out what is good in an idea. Moreover, I concluded, the positive story was going to be a far more important one in the long run.

The article that was eventually published in SUCCESS was the first fundamentally positive treatment of network marketing to appear in a major national publication. We pointed out how network marketing has often been wrongly confused with illegal pyramid schemes that convince people they can make money without working. We interviewed a range of experts, including Dr. Srikimar Rao, chairman of the marketing department at Long Island University and a student of MLM companies for nearly two decades. Dr. Rao began studying the field because he was aware that it had been ignored by mainstream researchers. Rao was one of the first academics to realize the enormous power of network marketing to create wealth. Our article also demonstrated how network marketing was being fueled by a pervasive sense of insecurity, an observation that seems more timely than ever today as we continue to witness tens of thousands of workers losing their jobs. Happily, many of these workers will find financial reward and personal freedom in network marketing.

Our conclusion was that network marketing was a powerful method of doing business that would grow in importance in the coming decade. The response to our coverage was so overwhelming that we have since made network marketing an ongoing part of our editorial coverage. Up to now, no book for the general public has appeared on the subject. So, the publication of *Future Choice* is a significant event.

Scott DeGarmo
Editor in Chief
SUCCESS Magazine

I N HIS BOOK, *All I Really Need to Know I Learned in Kindergar-ten*, author-philosopher Robert Fulghum tells the story of when Halley's Comet swept across our 1910 skies.

"The world was divided between those who celebrated and those who watched in fear and trembling," he said. Those who knew and understood the comet watched its fiery approach with awe and anticipation. Those who didn't watched in fear and dread. All experienced the same comet, but in completely different ways.

We believe we always have the opportunity to live our lives in the same two ways, in knowledgeable anticipation or in fear. Our choice shapes our future.

That's why we have chosen the comet to symbolize that choice and why we dedicate our book to the sense of anticipation in us all.

Our goal in *Future Choice* is to introduce you to one type of business opportunity -- network marketing. As you consider whether network marketing may be right for you, we hope we can in some small way help you to be among those who choose their future with knowledgeable anticipation.

1
2003,
A STORY

)

"By 1960, work will be limited to
three hours a day."
— John Langdon-Davies
A Short History of the Future, 1936

*Susan Edison leaned against the doorway as she looked
across the deck of her Colorado home to the meadows beyond.*

*She sighed with contentment, then turned back into the
house to grab her coffee cup as she moved through the kitchen
into the living room.*

*Speaking commands to her video home theater, Susan
quickly called up a hologram network and selected a style of sofa
she had been eyeing. Instantly, the form of the sofa appeared in
the room, in just the style and fabric she had requested.*

*Susan studied the three-dimensional sofa for a minute,
then shook her head a little and moved the theater's remote
control to position the hologram closer to the fireplace. A
double-click on the remote changed the sofa's fabric to one that
more closely reflected the shades of the wildflowers outside.*

Susan smiled. Just right.

*She moved the remote back to the video screen, clicked once
to order the sofa and again to request express home delivery.
Then, satisfied, she spoke a command to turn off the video*

display.

Although the sofa disappeared, Susan knew it would be delivered to her home in two days. And Jennifer Wellington, her dentist, would receive a commission on the sale.

In addition to her dental practice, Jennifer represented a company that offered a complete line of home furnishings. By buying her sofa through Jennifer's hologram network, Susan saved the cost of buying her furniture through the few retail stores that remained. Susan was able to support Jennifer, who in return was one of her own best customers.

Susan cast one last glance around her living room, pleased with the decisions she had made that morning, then moved across the hallway to her office. Only 10 minutes remained until her first conference of the day.

That morning Susan spoke with six of her top associates in a nationwide video conference call, addressed 1,500 new prospects through a two-way video link broadcast each Tuesday morning over her own personal channel on her company's satellite network and with a single push of a button sent her weekly newsletter by electronic mail to 30,000 of her own distributors.

Later, after lunch on the deck, Susan walked down into the meadow. The children would be home soon. This was her best chance for a few minutes to herself after a busy morning.

She'd come a long way in the last ten years, since 1993 when she had first opened her home-based business. All because she had listened to a friend who had told her about a new way of doing business.

I T MAY BE THE NEW AMERICAN DREAM, 1990s style. No boss, set your own hours, succeed or fail by your own efforts. All with a computer, a cordless phone and a fax machine. Preferably from a deck.

In a recent national survey, as many as 58 percent of those surveyed said they would like to start their own business, and record numbers are. Today, more than 28 million people work at home, full- or part-time, as business entrepreneurs or telecommuters. Millions of people design boats, make wine, create manuscripts or broker information from a spare corner in the garage or a spare room in the house.

Hewlett-Packard, Mrs. Fields' Cookies, Apple Computers, Domino's Pizza, Nike and Walt Disney Productions all started as home-based businesses, say Paul and Sarah Edwards, themselves home-based authors of a series of books on self-employment.

Whether one's dream is to catapult one's own company into the Fortune 500 or to blend home life and work life into one seamless existence, business forecasters say today's updated version of home-based entrepreneurship may be a model for the businesses of the future.

"There are two ways to the CEO's chair," write Patricia Aburdene and John Naisbitt in their book, *Megatrends for Women.* "The corporate route: draw up a five- or ten-year plan to gather the skills for the top-executive job you hope to land in, say, 1998 or 2003; and the entrepreneurial approach: start your own business now."

At the turn of the century, as many as 50 percent of U.S. adults were self-employed; by the turn of the next century, they may be again, the Edwardses predict.

Self-employment hit its low point in the late 1970s, at 7 percent. But by 1990, that number had climbed to 13 percent and by 1991, the number of self-employed in the U.S. had increased to 25 percent.

Several business trends are converging to spur a return to self-employment. One is the economy. As we continue the conversion from an industrial society to one based on information and services, the way Americans earn their living is changing as well. For too many of us, the change has been painful.

Fortune 500 companies shed 9 million jobs during the past decade. Companies such as General Motors, IBM and AT&T, once considered a ticket to lifelong employment security, are jettisoning middle-management layers and employees by the tens of thousands. In an effort to find a place in the evolving global economy, companies are selling off or closing down plants or entire divisions. They are centralizing and economizing, outsourcing and contracting. Entire industries are disappearing and taking with them the security of those who depended on them for a life's work.

As companies continue to consolidate operations, labor analysts say the number of corporate-based jobs will continue to decline. "The bond of loyalty between employer and employee has been broken by the merger mania and the 'lean and mean' response to global competition," writes Gerald Celente, a New York trends analyst in his book, *Trend Tracking.*

"If you work for a corporation, you can no longer sit back and enjoy the comfort of job security. If you're a top executive, you may have a golden parachute that will give you a nice soft landing. But if you're a senior executive, a middle manager or just an employee, you have nothing to protect you other than your ability to get a job somewhere else."

But where? And at what salary?

Many of yesterday's higher-paying manufacturing jobs now live overseas and still others are packing their bags for the trip. Since 1965, U.S. corporations have built more than 1,800 plants -- that employ more than 500,000 workers -- in neighboring Mexico alone. That figure is expected to climb to almost 3,000 plants by 1995, according to projections by the Secretariat of Commerce and

Industrial Development in Mexico City. While they say they regret the impact on U.S. workers, companies as diverse as Zenith and Fisher-Price say they have no choice but to move to countries where wage rates are lower if they want to remain competitive.

For the first time in our economic history, the cutbacks are slicing as deep into executive suites as production lines. Bank presidents, stock analysts and entire corporate public relations departments are as likely as a GM auto worker to find themselves suddenly unemployed.

Whatever the job classification, the contraction is not confined to marginal employees with limited skills. Today's unemployment lines are full of bright, motivated and engaging people -- people with much to offer. Unfortunately, the loss of their jobs is not temporary, nor is it part of a typical business cycle. Most of the jobs lost in the last decade will not return.

AMERICANS HAVE COME TO RELY on a three-legged financial stool to provide them with financial security -- a private pension, Social Security and personal savings. But for both men and women, that formula has all but disappeared. Personal debt remains at an all-time high and the U.S. national savings rate remains among the lowest in the industrialized world. Even workers who expect to receive a pension at retirement are not assured a comfortable life. Labor Department statistics show that in 1988 the median private pension for married men was $4,285 a year, or less than $83 a week; for single women it was $2,153 a year, or $41.40 a week.

The question is more than whether average pension rates are too low. It is whether those who have counted on a pension will actually receive one at all. According to the Federal Reserve and the Bureau of Labor Statistics, corporate debt climbed from $10,000 per employee in 1950 to $23,387 per employee by the end of the 1980s. Some companies took on the debt to finance a fight against corporate raiders; others were loaded with debt and stripped of assets after they fell victim. Either way, in a desperate search for cash to pay the interest on their debt, too many corporations went looking in the one place that was earlier sacrosanct -- their pension funds.

"Corporations removed $21 billion from their employees' pension plans during the 1980s; overall, nearly 2,000 corporations dipped into employee pension funds for at least $1 million each," say Philadelphia Inquirer investigative reporters Donald Barlett and James Steele in their Pulitzer Prize-winning book, *America: What Went Wrong?* When government moved to protect private pensions with laws that regulated pension-raiding, many companies made an end run around the new regulations by abandoning traditional corporate pensions altogether.

It seems the traditional three-legged stool of financial security has developed a marked wobble.

THAT WOBBLE IS ONE REASON millions of Americans are choosing to carve a new style of economic stool, one with four solid legs on the ground. The fourth leg is ownership of a full- or part-time business.

Record numbers of us are choosing to chart our own economic future, to live by our own business wits. By 1991, 38.4 million people were producing some type of income from their home. From 1980 to 1988, the number of entrepreneurs in the U.S. increased 56 percent.

Some of today's new business owners want to build an empire, like Walt Disney or Colonel Sanders. Others want only make a second income, one that will provide the difference between living and living well.

Financial experts say the quality of life of millions of Americans would increase significantly if they were able to increase their monthly income by only $200 to $500 a month. That is enough to start an investment account or to buy a more reliable car. It is enough to begin piano lessons, take the family to Disney World or pay off a credit card.

All this -- and more -- is possible. Because between today's economic uncertainty and Susan Edison, our 21st century entrepreneur, lies one of the business world's best kept secrets. And perhaps one of its most potent opportunities.

2

A Business
Of Your Own

")"

"Money can do good, great good...
Properly placed financial incentives
can get the best out of people. The
power of money steers medical
research and fuels the arts."
— Edward Hallowell, M.D. and
    William J. Grace, Jr., in *What Are You Worth?*

I N 1986, EUNICE VINBERG babysat part time in her home
to earn a little extra money. Today, not yet 30 years old,
she earns more than the president of the United States.
Much more. Her earnings just bought her family a sprawl-
ing new home in the suburbs of Seattle and her husband,
a youth pastor, now works because he loves his job, not
because he needs to.

The Vinbergs used spunk and energy to turn a
hot idea into a career -- the classic talent of a successful entrepreneur.

Eunice and Emil Vinberg are the top U.S. sales representatives for a California-based company that distributes
high-end Japanese skin care products and cosmetics. Noevir,
the second-largest direct-marketed company in Japan,

uses personal representatives to sell and distribute its products. The Vinbergs now work through a nationwide system of distributors that they, or those they sponsored, introduced to their company.

The Vinbergs are paid a commission on all their retail sales and a bonus on all sales in their organization. They make more money in a month than most people make in a year by introducing people to their company and by teaching and motivating others to duplicate their success.

"Somehow I knew if you got in with a company like this and it went big, you'd go to the top," said Marlee Huber, Eunice Vinberg's cousin, who after being introduced to the company by Eunice has developed her own widespread network of distributors.

Growing numbers of people like Marlee Huber and the Vinbergs are looking at the other side of today's global economic uncertainty, the opportunity side. Their home-based businesses allow them to take advantage of today's business trends, not fear them. They're building personal income and personal freedom using a business concept known today as network marketing.

NETWORK MARKETING, sometimes called multi-level marketing or MLM, is one of several ways to move products from manufacturers to consumers. Although network marketing is not a new concept, it is not well understood.

Network marketing is an alternative delivery system to those used by most major corporations in the U.S. today. While other more common forms of distribution are under stress -- witness the rash of bankruptcies in the retail industry -- network marketing is expanding rapidly. To illustrate why, let's take a look at some of the methods companies have developed to move their products. The most well known, of course, is the retail channel.

Companies spend enormous amounts of money, sometimes as much as $10 or $20 million per advertising campaign, to make you want to buy what they have to sell. Advertising may make you laugh or may make you grit your teeth, but if it gets you to leave your house in search of what a company is selling, it's a success.

Yet the cost of the advertising is just the beginning. Long before you've even warmed up your car, or before your children have badgered you into promising them the latest television-inspired fad, those companies have sold their products -- at a profit, of course -- to wholesalers and distributors across the country.

Wholesalers pay another entire layer of middlemen-- truckers and warehouse workers and clerical employees-- and then add their costs and their profit to the price of the item you want to buy. Your increasingly expensive product next moves into the retail store where, in many industries, wholesalers must pay an additional heavy fee to win the product a space on a retail shelf. That fee, like all the others, gets passed on to you. So does the cost of the store's advertising, its light bill and the cost of its employees' health insurance.

It should not surprise you if you, the shopper that all these people spent millions of dollars to attract, hear an almost audible sigh of relief across the U.S. retail landscape when you pull into a mall parking lot.

Yet you may not.

You may be too busy searching for a parking place or negotiating through a maze of store corridors specifically designed to confuse you. If you do reach your item, you then will wait in line to pay for it, balancing it in one hand while you attempt to reach for your two forms of identification with the other.

There must be a better way to make purchases, and consumers are searching for it.

Each week, millions of Americans travel to large discount warehouses where buying clubs offer rock bottom prices on mass merchandise to qualified members in exchange for an annual fee. They choose to trade service and convenience for value.

Others find they prefer shopping by catalog. A handful of large general department stores have operated giant catalog divisions for years. Their catalogs offer thousands of items for sale direct from the company's warehouses if they have your size, if the style you want isn't backordered and if you don't mind returning to the store four days later to pick it up.

Some specialty companies, such as L.L. Bean, have refined the art of shopping by catalog even further and market it as a more pleasant alternative to retail shopping.

Often known for the excellent service they provide, a number of catalog companies have developed followings of loyal customers who look forward to receiving each catalog. Their products often are of a quality and selection unavailable in most retail stores and their goods often are shipped to buyers' homes, satisfaction guaranteed.

Network marketing seeks to combine the best aspects of all the distribution systems -- the convenience of catalog shopping, the high quality merchandise offered by the best specialty shops and the cost savings of direct selling. Then it takes the concept one step further. Network marketing pays you to participate in its form of distribution.

SUCCESS Magazine calls network marketing "the most powerful way to reach consumers in the '90s." Dozens of the nation's most innovative companies are taking a second look at network marketing, because it is the one delivery method of goods and services that complements developing business trends.

"Manufacturers are looking for a way to spend advertising dollars as close to the point of sale as possible," says business author Charles Whitlock in his book, *How To Get Rich.*

"That's what network marketing does: it provides a one-on-one sales presentation to potential customers right at the point of sale. A person who wants to buy doesn't have to turn off the TV and go to the market, dial an 800 number or mail anything in. All the customer has to do is say yes. And the customer is likely to say yes, because MLM distributors are usually among the most enthusiastic and committed sales professionals in the marketplace today."

Today a consumer can buy almost anything through network marketing, from life insurance to health food. A number of the nation's corporations have built their business solely by network marketing. Other Fortune 500 companies have complete network marketing subsidiaries, including Colgate-Palmolive and Gillette. Rexall Drugs, one of the country's best-known retail names, has created a new division, Rexall Showcase International, to offer health and wellness products through a new network marketing arm. Other companies are creating partnerships with network marketing companies.

MCI and Sprint turned to Amway Corp. and Network 2000 to market their long distance services through those companies' nationwide networks of independent distributors. The joint venture worked. Three million subscribers later, AT&T, stung by the potency of network marketing, launched its "We want you back" advertising campaign.

SOME OF THE HIGHEST QUALITY and most innovative products over the years have been marketed solely through independent network distributors. Can openers, chewing gum, microwave ovens, razors, sewing machines, smoke detectors and vacuum cleaners all were first introduced into the marketplace through direct selling channels.

Business analysts predict the amount of goods and services that move through network channels will increase at a rate of as much as 30 percent per year in the next few years, many times the rate of growth predicted for the economy as a whole. Part of the reason is that the products most commonly marketed today through network marketing channels are those that will be appealing to the baby boom generation as it moves through middle age.

Trend trackers say baby boomers are searching for health, vitality, youthful appearances and convenience. They crave products that will make them healthy and attractive. They want quality products *and* perceived value. Yet they're willing to pay for what they want, even in lean times, because they feel they deserve it.

Internationally known futurist Faith Popcorn calls this trend "egonomics."

"It's about individuating, differentiating, customizing," she writes in her bestseller, *The Popcorn Report.* "And it's a major force to reckon with in today's marketplace. Egonomics means simply this: there is profit to be reaped in providing for the consumer's need for personalization, whether it be in product concept, product design, or personal service."

Network marketing companies have been on the forefront of those trends for years with all-natural food supplements, organically grown packaged food, herbal cosmetic and skin care lines and earth friendly recyclable packaging. As this massive group of consumers moves into the most vibrant and active middle years yet known to humankind, networking companies await with products to help them retain their zest, lose excess weight, fight wrinkles and insure their lives.

According to Popcorn's research, in the decade of the

1990s people also are retrenching. They see the frenzy in their lives and they are looking for ways to build a more serene and prosperous future for themselves and those they love. They are searching for ways to build that future without sacrificing themselves to the process. It's a movement that authors Patricia Aburdene and John Naisbitt call the search for opportunity, leadership and balance. It is a search for ways to work smarter, live smarter and choose smarter so there is more left to give to families, to the world and to one another. It is a desire to create something of value and integrity with which to shape a future of joy and prosperity.

For millions of Americans, network marketing offers that opportunity.

ONE PLUS

ONE

)

"Leisure time, not money, is becoming
the status symbol of the 1990s."
— John P. Robinson,
      University of Maryland researcher

I N 1991, DARRYL AND LYNN KUNTZ of Rockwall, Texas,
were living the new American dream.
They had made the leap that small business advocates
Paul and Sarah Edwards had predicted, to a home-based
business of their own. As successful movie producers, the
Kuntzes specialized in family movies and videos for
national distribution. Lynn Kuntz wrote the script for their
largest production, *"Dakota"*, a movie that opened nationwide in 1988 starring Lou Diamond Phillips.

They worked from twin offices in their lakeside country home. Their business allowed them to work together
and to be deeply involved with their four children, yet by
the early 1990s Darryl and Lynn had decided they needed
to rethink the direction of their business. Each movie
project meant raising millions of dollars from investors and
as a recession darkened the nation, investment capital was
becoming harder to find.

"We were looking to diversify," Lynn Kuntz said. "We

were especially interested in residual income. We sat down and tried to think what qualities we would look for in a second business.

"We had been in business for a number of years," she said. "We knew the amount of paperwork involved, the time devoted to keeping track of taxes and accounting. We were looking for something that would not include the 'busyness' of a small business. We wanted something that would allow us to work together -- Darryl and I have always worked together -- and we wanted something with the potential to go big. If you're going to invest your time and effort, you want the opportunity to find the gold at the end of the rainbow. We were looking for something that was seemingly impossible."

Perhaps not.

A wealthy business associate who had been an investor in their film projects introduced them to network marketing. "We called him and asked him if we could attend one of his meetings," Lynn said. "We made it clear we were not interested in his company. We were considering whether we would be able to develop a network marketing program to distribute our films.

"We went, and we were so impressed when we realized what the business trends were and what the income potential was." That night, the Kuntzes realized that network marketing met all their criteria for an additional business venture. Not long after the meeting, the Kuntzes discovered a company that distributes high technology skin care products developed by a world-renowned scientist. After thoroughly investigating the company, its products and leadership, the Kuntzes joined. Today their "downline," those to whom they have introduced the concept, is one of their company's fastest growing groups.

As experienced business people, the Kuntzes took a clear, close look at network marketing before deciding it was the opportunity they sought. "We were not looking for this at all," Lynn Kuntz said. "We've been surprised at how much we enjoy this business. We consider ourselves creative people, and there are so many creative ways to build our business. We don't feel we have put our creativity aside at all."

The Kuntzes have been approached about other film projects, but for now they have decided to build their network business.

"We feel like the ball is really rolling with this now," Lynn Kuntz said. "We believe we'll be able to build an income that will allow us to finance our own films sometime in the future. But it's not like we're working at this until we're able to do what we really want. We love this. Someday later on we may decide to do a film project. We'll do both."

THE KUNTZES ARE NOT ALONE in their move into network marketing. The Direct Selling Association, one of several industry associations, estimates $12.96 billion of goods and services were sold by network companies in 1991, up more than $1 billion in only one year. In 1991, more than 5 million people are estimated to have earned an income from network marketing, an increase of more than 400,000 people in one year alone.

"I used to think the only way to succeed was to climb the corporate ladder," said Bill Hayden, owner of a networking business, to Richard Poe, a senior editor of SUCCESS Magazine. "But when I found out about MLM, I willingly gave up my six-figure income as a mortgage banker."

The first experience many have with network marketing is when they are approached by someone they know with an opportunity to buy products from a company they represent. Millions of Americans have purchased products or services from a network entrepreneur. Even if they make purchases at first primarily to show support for a friend's new business venture, they often later find themselves returning when they discover the value and quality of the products and services.

There are three common ways to participate in network marketing:

1. As a wholesale buyer. Most of those involved in network marketing sign up with a company only to buy its products wholesale. Wholesale buyers purchase products primarily for themselves and their families. Typically, they pay a nominal annual fee, much like the membership fees charged by wholesale buying clubs, to buy their products at a reduced cost directly from the company itself or from their "sponsor," the person who introduced them to the company.

2. As a part-time networker. Like wholesale buyers, part-time networkers buy and use their company's products for themselves and their families. In addition, they also, even on a casual basis, tell some of their friends, neighbors or relatives about their savings. They introduce a few others to the company and help them sign up to receive the same product discounts. They then receive a bonus, typically a small percentage of the total sales of everyone they sponsor into the company's marketing program.

Even networkers who go on to earn large monthly bonuses, like the Vinbergs who opened our chapter, typically begin as wholesale buyers or as part-time networkers. In a 1992 survey, the Direct Selling Association estimated that almost 90 percent of all networkers work at their business only part-time.

Part-time networkers can expect to build incomes of from $200 to $500 a month or more as their networks grow, experienced networkers say. Those who build size-able networks or who sponsor others who do can earn incomes many times that.

Thousands of part-time network professionals are matching -- sometimes many times -- the salaries they earn at their full-time jobs.

"People will get started in a multi-level business with the idea of making $50, $100 or even $200 per month and suddenly they will realize that if they want to get serious about the business, they could be making $1,000 or $2,000 per month or more," writes premier network trainer Don Failla in his book, *How to Build a Large, Successful Multi-Level Marketing Organization.*

3. *As a full-time networker.* Those who decide to build a full-time network marketing business buy and use their company's products for themselves and their families. In addition, they work full-time to tell others about their company, its products and the business opportunity it presents.

"When I first signed up with Mary Kay, reactions ranged from doubtful to very, very doubtful," recounts Shirley Hutton in her book, *Pay Yourself What You're Worth.* Hutton moved from a career in television as host of a TV talk show to representing industry giant Mary Kay Cosmetics.

"My husband thought I'd lost my mind, my daughter Elizabeth was shocked and the other three children more or less snickered," she said. "Within the first three months, Shirley Hutton saw more gaped jaws than any dentist."

But not for long. In the first few years of Hutton's new venture, her income rose to more than $400,000 a year.

Network marketing's advantage is its ability to com-pensate company representatives not only for their own work, but also for the work of those they bring into the company, even into second and third and subsequent levels of participation. Network marketed companies use the money more traditional companies spend on advertising and distribution to pay commissions and bonuses to their representatives, to those who are taking their products directly to the market place.

It's called the exponential success path. And it is open to any network marketer -- wholesale, part-time or full-time -- sometimes with astounding results. Network marketers across the country are earning $10,000, $20,000, $50,000 and more. Per month.

NETWORKERS USE TWO FAVORITE EXAMPLES to explain networking's exponential compensation system. The first is called the doubling concept. Here's an example:

Take one penny and set it aside. The next day, and every day thereafter, double the number of pennies you set aside.

It's simple. On the second day, you will have two cents; on the third day, four cents. By the end of the first week, you will have 64 cents. Now fasten your financial seat belt.

By the end of the second week, you will have accumulated $81.92. By the end of the third week, more than $10,000 and by the end of the month, you will have saved well over $5 million and will be scrambling for storage space for all those pennies. Turn the pennies into people bearing bonuses and turn the days into weeks or months, and the economic power of network marketing begins to emerge.

Here's how doubling might work in real life, using network marketing's second common example:

Suppose that after learning about the power of network marketing and finding a company whose products you believe in, you pay a nominal fee -- usually under $50 -- to become a distributor.

In the first month, you tell your friends and family about your new venture and about the exciting benefits of the products you represent. You are able to save money buying the products you use at wholesale prices, and you make an immediate profit by selling some products at retail prices to those who want to buy directly from you.

Now suppose that, in addition, you find one person who would like to join you, someone who also recognizes the potential of network marketing and who wants to do what you are doing.

At the end of your first month, you would be saving money by purchasing your products wholesale, making profits from your own retail sales *and* earning bonuses on all the sales of the person you sponsored into the organization.

That's the beginning of what network marketers call a "downline." You have two people in your organization -- yourself and your first sponsored colleague. One plus one makes two (see *Figure 1*). Maybe.

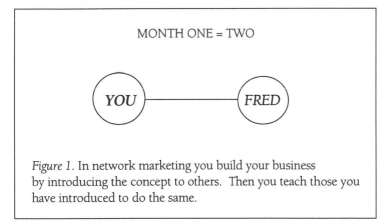

MONTH ONE = TWO

Figure 1. In network marketing you build your business by introducing the concept to others. Then you teach those you have introduced to do the same.

To continue the example, what if in the second month you sponsor one other person into your organization? And the person you sponsored sponsors one person. Suddenly you have four people in your organization and you're earning bonuses on the sales of all those people, yet you yourself sponsored only two people *(see Figure 2)*.

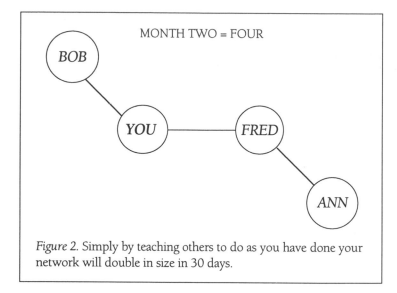

Figure 2. Simply by teaching others to do as you have done your network will double in size in 30 days.

Again, in the third month of your business, you sponsor one person. So do each of those already in your group. Now you've grown to eight: you, the three people you have sponsored directly and the four others they have introduced to your business. Remember, this all could be happening before most other startup businesses have earned a single profit *(see Figure 3)*.

To show the true power of network marketing, let's follow the example a little further.

Suppose you, as a part-time or full-time network entrepreneur, decide to find more than one person a month to join you in your business. Suppose instead of just one person, you sponsor two people each month who want to build a business as you are.

You sponsor two people the first month, who sponsor two the next, who teach their two to sponsor two. By the end of four months, you have 30 active people in your

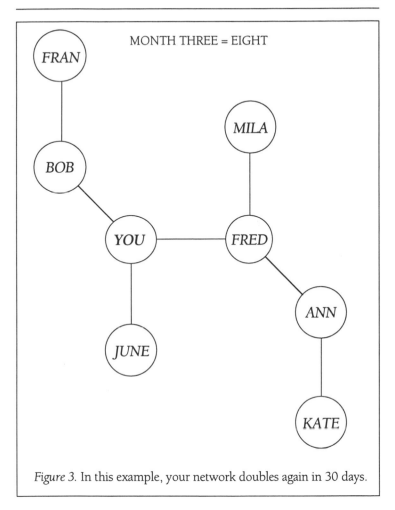

MONTH THREE = EIGHT

Figure 3. In this example, your network doubles again in 30 days.

group, yet you yourself have sponsored only one more person each month.

Take the examples two steps further.

If you, as a serious builder, sponsor four people each month with similar ambitions, by the end of four months you will enjoy a network of 256 committed business builders. If you sponsor five, that number explodes to 625. Yet you personally sponsor only five people each month.

Now here's where your efforts turn into income.

In network marketing, you receive compensation, called a bonus, from the sale of all products within your group. If each of your 625 people buys only $100 worth of products per month to use personally, to share as gifts and to show to others, you and your group will have sold $62,500 worth of products. Your bonus check could easily reach above $7,000, depending on the compensation plan of your company.

If each person in your group buys only $50 worth of products or services each month, that still totals $31,250, which could well bring you more than $3,000 a month. Remember, that's without any barn burners, any extra-achievers or any large amount of retail sales. That's you and five of your colleagues teaching those you sponsor to build their organizations just as you have yours (see *Figure 4*) .

Figure 4. Look what would happen if you introduced five people into your business and taught each one to do the same. *At the end of four months, you would have almost 800 people in your network.*

	Total number in your group	
YOU		
TEACH FIVE	(5)	6
HOW TO TEACH FIVE	(25)	31
TO EACH SPONSOR FIVE	(125)	156
WHO WILL EACH SPONSOR FIVE	(625)	781

Network marketers across the country are using concepts just like these to build substantial incomes for themselves and their families. As we continue, let's look more closely at how.

PROFITS &

PROSPERITY

"In the 90s, instead of going to the store,
the store will come to us."
— Faith Popcorn
The Popcorn Report

EVEN WHEN HE WAS YOUNG, anyone who knew Dayle
Maloney knew he was someone in a hurry. A paper
route wasn't enough for young Dayle. Before he had
graduated from school, he owned and operated his own
concession stand. Unfortunately, before Dayle could get to
where he really wanted to go, to a career as a sports coach,
polio ended his dreams. His doctors told him he would
never walk again without aid.

But Dayle didn't listen. He fought back with extra
treatments and an undefeatable optimism. Dayle recovered
from his illness and went on to own several successful
businesses before turning his attention to network marketing. Today, as a nationwide leader, he travels the country
training and motivating those in his group. Since 1986, his
networking income has grown from $200,000 a year to
$800,000.

How is that possible?

Leading networkers across the country are making

$10,000, $20,000, $75,000 per month by putting two concepts, exponential growth and indirect compensation, to work in their businesses.

As we described earlier, all network marketing companies compensate their representatives through some form of exponential bonus payment. As a distributor, you receive commissions on your sales and bonuses on all sales in your group. Your income grows as the amount of product sold by members of your group grows. Your compensation is directly linked to your efforts, not to some artificial outside evaluation of how much your skills and talents are worth, as is often the case with a traditional salary. There is no limit to how well your efforts can be rewarded. There are no salary freezes or caps, no waiting to see if your company will offer a production bonus. Office politics play no part in your compensation; neither does favoritism.

With indirect compensation, you once again profit not only from your own work, but from the work of a growing number of others, as well. You're on the same team, and joint team goals build strong partnerships. *You* benefit from the work of your associates; you all benefit from the effort *you* contribute.

As you learn your business, you teach, coach and motivate the other members of your team. They become more effective businesses owners in their own right and all of you experience greater prosperity and higher levels of accomplishment. As their businesses grow, they do the same with their teams. They continue your legacy of success and you all continue to prosper.

Once you establish your network, you can go on vacation, care for a sick child, visit family, go on a second honeymoon or decide to just swing in a hammock for a while and your business will continue to grow.

Some time ago, Linda Litle of Bozeman, Montana,

leader of a rapidly growing group, won a trip to Japan through her company. Her husband, a physician, could not leave his practice to accompany her, yet when she returned from her trip her business had doubled because those in her group had been working while she was away. Her husband, meanwhile, had worked long hours just to maintain his patient load.

"That's when my husband said, 'Hey, I'd better look at this,' " she said.

THE EXACT FORMULA BY WHICH a network marketing company rewards its distributors is called a marketing plan. Marketing plans vary according to company. Each includes different requirements and compensation methods, based on the company's products, its philosophy, the customer base it is trying to reach and its vision of the future.

Some plans encourage representatives to build their organizations wide, that is, to sponsor many people directly. Others provide the greatest compensation to those who build deep, who sponsor a few people at a time and then teach them to sponsor others in a similar way.

In addition to commissions based on retail sales and bonuses awarded for group sales, most plans provide additional compensation by increasing the discount on products as you advance through the organization. For instance, according to one type of plan, you may buy your product from Anna, your sponsor, for 20 percent off retail. You then are able to make an instant 20 percent profit by re-selling those products at their retail price.

At the same time, Anna, because she has more people in her group, may be eligible to buy her products from Ben, her sponsor, for 30 percent off the retail price. She makes a 10 percent profit on what she sells to you and 30 percent on any products she retails herself. Ben, in turn, may receive 40 percent off his products from Carl, who buys from the company for 50 percent off.

In another type of plan, all distributors buy their products at wholesale prices directly from the company, yet as the amount of product moving through their group grows, distributors may become eligible for even deeper discounts.

Don't be deceived by skeptics who say that compensation plans based on exponential growth are sure to implode under the weight of their own development. It's true that, carried to its extreme, the concept of exponential growth would, at least on paper, have everyone signed up as a distributor to some company in short order, leaving no one for those who enter late to sponsor.

That's not going to happen. Not everyone wants to begin a networking business. The timing may not be right for one or more of a hundred reasons. Some will never be interested in the concept. Others join a company and then drop out when they don't find a way to get rich quick or a quick-fix solution to whatever problems confront them.

EXPERIENCED NETWORKERS SAY those who begin part-time, who take the time to learn their business and who make a commitment to stick to it can expect to earn from several hundred to several thousand dollars per month. The opportunity for full-time networkers is unlimited, depending on the time, energy and skill they bring to their work. Yet no matter what the compensation level, prosperity is more than a bonus check, and networking offers additional, equally tangible rewards:

--*Tax advantages*. As owner of your own home-based business, you may be eligible for potent tax advantages and retirement savings. Check carefully with your accountant.

Many of the costs of doing business are tax deductible, even if the people you are doing business with are family and friends.

--Small initial investment. You can begin your business with a small initial investment. Today, for example, franchises provide one of the most popular ways to be self-employed. But franchises can cost from $10,000 to $1 million and inventory and equipment can cost as much again or more.

Most franchise owners begin their new ventures under a load of debt. For their investment, they receive the right to use the name of a well-known company, along with company support and training in a proven method of operation. Those are the very same things you, as owner of your own network marketing business, will receive from your company and your sponsor, usually for less than $100.

--Low overhead. As a network marketer, you can begin your business immediately with no overhead, no leases, no employees and no contracts. With no accounts receivable and little or no inventory. Some companies are so sophisticated that all paperwork, even collection and distribution of sales tax, is handled directly from the company. You assume only responsibility for making sure your home-based business meets state and local regulations.

--Immediate profits. Business consultants say most small start-up businesses should be prepared to lose money for as long as a year, as they build their customer base. You, on the other hand, are poised for immediate profit because you pay for your own growth out of business profits. As a business owner, you may find you enjoy greater standing in your business community. Small business owners are one of the most powerful segments in today's economy; they provide the majority of our nation's employment opportunities.

--*Flexible hours.* If you are already employed, you can begin your business while you retain your present job. Ninety percent of network marketers work their businesses part-time. Many of today's network leaders began building their businesses with an investment of only a few hours each week. You are free to fit your work around your life, not your life around your work. You can arrange your business hours so you can be available to your children, your parents and your friends, and you can choose with whom you work. You build your organization to include those who add enjoyment and satisfaction to your life; your customers are people you already care about and those you meet along the way to greater achievement.

Some find they enjoy their new business so much that they simply decide to grow it large enough to allow it to become their primary source of income. Others turn to their network marketing business when they lose their regular job. And some decide early to commit to becoming a network leader. Their dream is to build a significant income, one that allows them total financial security and freedom.

All these business building strategies are possible. The advantage of network marketing is that you decide how you want to grow your business. And you decide when to change that strategy.

--*Family time.* Your new business may even offer a chance to get to know your family better. "A moonlight business happens to be especially suited for family enterprises because of the obvious built-in support and mutual assistance afforded by members of the family: a built-in, already functioning combination of interests," writes Philip Holland in *How to Start a Business Without Quitting Your Job.* "The business will produce not only collective income, but also the opportunity to work in harmony for a common cause. Indeed, the economic interdependence of a family business can become the cohesive remedy for the splintered nature of contemporary family life."

Yet even with all the above tangible advantages, the most powerful reward may be one that comes from within. As a business owner, you are free to chart your own course to success. You, with guidance and support from your sponsor and company, decide how to build your business. Your time is your own. No boss looks over your shoulder; you punch no time clock.

"Playing the role of entrepreneur can provide a marvelous contrast from the frustrations inherent in salaried jobs," Holland says. "It will offset the muddy compromises one must wade through when working for others. It will provide the opportunity for self-realization that eludes us at work. The exercise of final authority will revitalize your mental and physical powers and tap into a reservoir of strength unrealized during the absence of opportunity. Being president is exhilarating and can properly be described as the sweetest morsel in the candy store."

OF SCOUNDRELS

AND VISIONARIES

———————

"Stocks have reached what looks
like a permanently high plateau."
— Irving Fisher, Professor of Economics
Yale University, Oct. 17, 1929

I F NETWORK MARKETING is such a powerful way to build
individual wealth, why aren't the world's business
leaders talking more about it? Why haven't we learned
about this concept from a professor of economics instead of
from our best friend's sister?

That's the magic of network marketing.

Remember, companies who choose to distribute their
goods and services through network marketers don't have
to spend millions of dollars on prime time advertisements,
Sunday morning "infomercials" or enough direct mailers
and magazine ads to doom several national forests. You
won't hear about it on television or from professional
economists.

Instead, network marketing relies on the oldest, most
powerful advertising medium ever devised -- word of
mouth. Mike tells a business colleague, Sam, about his new
part-time venture. Sam becomes intrigued and tells Judith,

his doctor. Judith, seeing the success Sam begins to enjoy, becomes involved and tells her brother and her stockbroker. At the end of just that one chain of events, Mike finds himself working with four new business builders, receiving bonuses from all their sales and from all those who follow them. Mike's business grows from one conversation with a co-worker.

Yet just because it is not yet taught in Harvard Business School does not mean network marketing is not a powerful economic force with its own rich history.

"The concept of using a geometric progression to establish control within an organization, or to pass along information, has been present for centuries," writes Michael Harden in his 1987 study of network marketing, *The Handbook of Multi-Level Marketing.*

"Before the written word, primitive societies would pass legends, stories and other tribal information on to younger members of the tribe. They, in turn, would pass the information on to the next generation. Of course, as this process continued with each generation, new information and stories were added, thereby increasing each generation's knowledge."

THROUGHOUT THE CENTURIES network marketing, like all powerful concepts, has evolved. Like all economic systems, it has been molded through the years by geniuses and scoundrels, by visionaries and an occasional huckster.

One of the first modern uses of the concept of exponential growth to generate income may have been the chain letter craze that swept the U.S. after World War I. The letters promised great profit if you would just send a dime -- or sometimes a dollar -- to the person at the top of the list and add your name to the bottom.

The chain letters spread as far as Europe and by the

mid-1930s, the U.S. post office estimated that 10 million letters were being mailed each day, even as postal authorities and law enforcement agencies battled the fraudulent schemes. The chain letter phenomenon began to subside in the early 1940s, although school girls and an occasional adult may still receive a version, usually without the unlawful request for money.

Modern network marketing is almost 50 years old. Then still more commonly known as multi-level marketing, it began in the early 1940s with the NutraLite Food Supplement Corp. "Like many truly innovative breakthroughs," the development of true network marketing was an accident, writes David Stewart in his 1991 book *Network Marketing: An Action Guide for Success.*

NutraLite, a company that offered food supplements, originally was organized as a direct selling company. Independent distributors would buy its products and resell them directly to consumers. But, according to Stewart, Nutralite's products proved to be so popular and beneficial that the company found consumers were recommending them to their friends and becoming distributors "based on their enjoyment of the product's benefits and a desire for additional income. That was a far cry from the cold-calling on strangers, hype and high-pressure techniques employed by door-to-door and conventional sales," Stewart writes.

In 1943, NutraLite restructured its marketing program to encourage each of its distributors to build -- and be compensated for -- their own individual sales organizations. Distributors were to receive bonuses on product sales made by those they sponsored, through a certain number of levels.

In 1956, NutraLite was joined in network marketing by Dr. Forrest Shaklee, who founded a company to gain wider distribution of the food supplements he had developed in his clinic. Over the years, Shaklee would grow to include more than a million North American distributors who offer almost 150 products.

Not long after, in 1959, former NutraLite distributors Rich DeVoss and Jay VanAndel drew on the words American and "way of doing business" to name their own new personal and household products company Amway. Shaklee and Amway, two of network marketing's true pioneers, paved the way for a new form of business.

Unfortunately, that pavement proved slippery for a handful of scoundrels more interested in getting rich quick than in operating legitimate businesses. As entrepreneurs rushed to adopt this new form of distribution, some overstepped the bounds of ethical business practices. Mutated forms of multi-level marketing turned into schemes designed to reward distributors solely for signing up others, not for marketing legitimate products. Some companies forced distributors to pay huge up-front fees or hidden charges for questionable reasons. Other fast-talkers entered the arena, reaped quick sign-up fees and then disappeared. These schemes came to be known as pyramids, because they often rewarded those first enticed into the organization, to the detriment of those who joined later.

In 1974, Sen. Walter Mondale declared such companies to be the nation's number one consumer fraud. Companies such as Koscot Interplanetary, Holiday Magic and Bestline Products were shut down.

Law enforcement agencies moved quickly to clean up the abuses. In the mid-1970s, burned by illegitimate schemes and scoundrels -- and with still no clear idea of what constituted a legitimate use of multi-level marketing -- the Federal Trade Commission and state agencies across the nation turned their wary eyes to almost all multi-level companies. In 1975, the FTC filed suit against Amway, alleging that the company was an illegal pyramid and that its refusal to sell its products in retail stores constituted a restraint of trade.

Amway spent four years and millions of dollars in legal fees to clear its name. In 1979, the FTC ruled that Amway was not a pyramid, that it did generate substantial revenue from the sale of its products to consumers. In addition, the FTC acknowledged that Amway had "built a substantial manufacturing company and an efficient distribution system," according to Michael Harden's account of the settlement.

Amway and other multi-level companies that fought to prove their legitimacy won important victories for network marketing. Network marketing exploded in the next decade, as companies entered a newly vindicated industry.

"Every industry goes through an evolution," said Kelly Thayer, who in 1992 was named one of INC. Magazine's regional entrepreneurs of the year. Thayer and his company, Clear Image, Inc., produce presentation videos for many of the top U.S. network marketing companies.

"In the 1960s as franchising was emerging, it was looked on as a scam, yet today more than 60 percent of all businesses are franchises," Thayer said. "Chiropractors were called the quacks of the 1970s. And look at the stock market; in the early days, the stock market was considered shady. All concepts run their course; they work the bugs out. In the decade of the 90s, you will see network marketing become the preferred way of marketing products."

The struggles in the early years of network marketing made important contributions to its future. They defined the ethics and standards by which the network marketing industry governs itself today. Government and industry officials continue to keep a close eye on questionable ventures that seem to search out the law's gray areas or look for loopholes in today's ethics and standards. That increase in credibility is one reason for network marketing's growth.

"Today we're seeing a change in the people attracted to this industry," said attorney Hugh Clemmons, Jr., in the video *Network Marketing*. "They demand more ethics and professionalism from the companies and they're refusing to do business with companies that don't live up to those expectations."

NETWORK MARKETING HAS EVOLVED in other ways, as well.

Many of today's network companies began as direct selling companies, in which independent distributors sold primarily to a large number of retail customers. Examples include Avon Products Inc., The Fuller Brush Co. and Encyclopaedia Britannica North America. In the last few years, however, many direct selling companies have switched to network marketing.

They found they still were able to get their products directly to their customers without the dreaded "s-" word because, when asked, more than 95 percent of people will say either that they *can't* sell or they *hate* to sell.

Because network marketers build their networks of customers from among those they already know or those they meet as they go about their activities -- that word-of-mouth concept, again -- they do not make "cold-calls" to strangers. They sponsor only those who may be interested and then teach them to continue the process.

One other reason for the decline of direct selling is that, beginning in the 1970s and continuing today, when distributors made those cold calls, no one was home. Women, long the customer backbone of direct sales, had entered the workforce in astounding numbers, leaving few behind to buy brushes and encyclopedias and cosmetics.

Even companies who emphasized party plans, in which a "hostess" would gather a few of her friends for a presentation by an independent distributor, suffered. After a day at work, few women had the time or inclination to venture out again in the evening, even for what was usually billed as a social evening with friends.

Companies watching these societal trends moved quickly to revise their marketing plans to allow for other, more informal, methods of sale. According to the DSA, in 1992 only 11.6 percent of sales took place in party or group settings, down from 21 percent in 1988. More than 70 percent of 1992 sales were from one individual to another, one-to-one. Although 81.6 percent of 1992 sales were transacted in the home, it most likely was on a more informal basis rather than a traditional sales call. And the percentage of sales taking place in the workplace has grown from 11.7 percent in 1988 to almost 13 percent in 1992.

NETWORK MARKETING HAS GROWN in the years since the 1979 Amway vindication, in both size and stature. Today's companies represent products and services that include those on the forefront of innovation and imagination, products that often are not available anywhere else. Network marketers are leading the way with healthful, natural and earth-friendly products, products that today are bringing us healthier and more rewarding lives.

Millions of independent businessmen and women are representing their companies with integrity and grace. And they're reaping the rewards.

6

YOUR

GRADUATE EDUCATION

"All you need to win is an understanding of the rules and of how the game is played."
— Michael S. Clouse

Susan Edison pushed herself back from the computer console in her office and laughed out loud, at herself and at the vision of her friend Geoffrey on the screen in front of her.

Geoffrey grinned back at her.

"There's no way I'm going to make it to the Cape by Friday," he said. "My in-basket is leaning like the Tower of Pisa. I could be crushed at any moment. We'll be lucky if we make it by Sunday afternoon. How long are you staying? Theresa and I need to get back by the 15th. We're starting a new group in New Orleans and I promised to set up training sessions there by the end of the month."

"No problem," Susan said. "The kids and I are coming out on Tuesday, but Tom won't make it until the weekend, either. But we are going to stay for a few weeks. As long as I have a power source, I can keep in touch as well there as here."

"Great," Geoffrey said. "We'll get a chance for a real visit. I'll get started on this list of ideas and beam you a progress report tomorrow. Hey, and give Andy a call, would you? He says Samantha has big news." With a wave, Geoffrey disappeared

from the screen.

Susan laughed again. What a pair.

She never would have guessed Geoffrey and Andy would become such good friends. They were so different...

Geoffrey was her banker when she had first started her business. He was a shrewd businessman, and he had watched the bank mergers and consolidations of the 1990s with a wary eye. When his community bank was bought out by a financial corporation in 1994, he took advantage of the bank's early retirement offer to its middle management. As he had brainstormed new career ideas, he remembered Susan's success and gave her a call to talk about the opportunities in network marketing.

Geoffrey had been a fast starter from the first.

He had used his ability to read people, his firsthand knowledge of people's worries about financial insecurity and a high energy level to spread the word about his company's products and opportunities. Before the end of his second year in business, he had matched his former bank salary, and by the end of his third year, he had doubled it. Today, he earned enough to not only insure his family's future, but to allow them to enjoy their time together now.

But Andy!

Andy had joined Susan about the same time as Geoffrey. He had been a young man with a good, steady job. When he talked with Susan he told her he and his wife Samantha were looking for a second income, something that would allow them to provide their young children with a few of the extras in life. The trouble was, between their jobs, the children and Andy's elderly parents, neither had much time to devote to any additional venture.

Even so, together with Susan they had mapped out a few extra hours a week. Susan assured them that many people are able to build substantial part-time businesses in network marketing by committing only five or 10 or 15 hours a week (see

Appendix B).

Andy and Samantha took her at her word and went to work.

They told their friends, their family and their co-workers about their new business and introduced them to their company's products. When their friends and family found they could substitute the products they were now using with ones of higher quality -- and discovered they would be delivered directly to their door -- some began to buy from Andy and Samantha at retail prices. That meant an immediate profit for the fledgling business.

Others, after trying some of the products, decided they wanted to buy them at wholesale prices directly from the company. That saved them money and earned Andy and Samantha a bonus every time someone placed an order.

One by one, over time, those they introduced to their company told others about the products and opportunities. As new people joined, Andy and Samantha's group grew. So did their monthly bonus checks.

Neither of them quit their job. They didn't take out a loan to pay for business start-up costs. And they sure didn't have to leave their children with baby sitters to build their business. They simply told the people they knew -- and those they met as they went about their day -- about their company and its products. Some were interested enough to try the products. Some weren't. Some wanted to know more about the new business. Others never asked for more information.

Andy and Samantha didn't get rich quick. But by the time they had worked at their new business for a few months, they knew they were making progress toward their goals. They enjoyed sharing their discovery with those they knew. And although their bonus checks were small, they knew they were building the foundation for their success.

Then something began to happen.

Samantha's Uncle Mike in Detroit bought one of the

products. He introduced it to his buddies at work, who told their relatives, and suddenly Andy and Samantha had a hot group growing in Detroit. A couple of months later, Andy's sister's best friend in Baton Rouge lost her job and decided to take her part-time network marketing business more seriously. By the end of the year, she was head of one of the fastest growing groups in the company and Andy and Samantha were shopping for tax shelters.

Now, eight years later, Geoffrey and Andy are golfing buddies with plans to start a snorkeling equipment company in the Bahamas, just for fun. They are two of Susan's top associates, yet each chose a different path to get them there. Geoffrey started out fast, and his success seemed to come just as rapidly. Andy and Samantha, with help from Susan and their company, built their business at their own pace. They took time along the way to watch their children grow and to care for Andy's mother. Even so, only a few years later, their business provided them with much more than the extras they had first hoped for. It allowed them a life they had only dreamed of before. All by working a few consistent extra hours a week with family, with friends and with friends of friends.

N O TWO NETWORK MARKETING COMPANIES are alike. Compensation plans differ, as do products and business philosophies. Each company has a different personality and a different focus. Some extremely reputable companies are flamboyant, others are more businesslike. Each approaches its product development, its distributor community and its business decisions a little differently. Even so, top-class network companies share several important characteristics. They adhere to the industry's highest principles and codes of ethics (see *Appendix C*). They value their distributor community and they constantly look for ways to improve both their services and their products.

If you choose to become a network business owner, your choice of company will be one of your most important decisions. Look for:

1. Company experience in network marketing. Other business experience is good, but you are looking for experience in network marketing. Network marketing is an alternate method of product distribution. It also is a very different way to structure a company. Make sure the company you select has been in business long enough to prove it knows what it's doing. Many of the here-today, gone-tomorrow companies that fly through the network marketing community simply didn't know what they were getting into.

2. Company in business at least three years. There's a philosophy in network marketing that says if you get in on the ground floor of a hot new company, you'll rise to the top as it grows. Perhaps. But for every true opportunity, there are at least a dozen companies that come on strong, then fizzle and fade, leaving their distributors with downlines but no company. Better to catch the elevator on the second or third floor and ride the rest of the way to the top.

Look for a company that has at least a strong three year track record of success. Five years would be better. A ground floor opportunity is a risky venture. Make sure your ground floor opportunity is built on a strong foundation.

3. Strong financial base. More companies in all types of business fail because of lack of financial depth than all other reasons put together. Network marketing companies, especially young ones, are under particular stress. They can grow rapidly, straining their ability to finance their growth responsibly. It takes a steady management hand on the wheel to chart a course between the rapid growth of networking and a solid balance sheet for the future.

4. Top-flight company management and professionalism. You want that hand at the wheel to know which way it needs to steer. You want your company's management to be experienced, inventive, creative and professional. Check to see if the company you are considering is a member of an industry association such as the Direct Selling Association or the Multi-level Marketing International Association. For example, many of network marketing's top companies belong to the DSA. Those who join undergo close scrutiny and a membership waiting period, and they agree to adhere to the association's strict code of ethics.

5. Company commitment to distributors. The company you want to work for values its distributors. It constantly is looking for ways to improve its products, the way it does business and its ability to help you do your job and build your business. It knows what you need and helps you get it. Quality companies know their success depends on your success and they're there, offering training, support, education and encouragement. You need to know that your company is committed to your success and to its future as a network marketing company.

6. Professional-quality presentation tools. "I've found the business opportunity of a lifetime," a friend tells you. "You've *got* to take a look at this. Easy Street, here I come." Then he hands you a faded and crinkled copy of a copy of a copy. What are the chances you'll take him seriously?

Before you sign on any enrollment line, make sure your company has the tools you will need to make your business a success. Tools like business cards and professional-looking and informative product catalogs and brochures. Perhaps a company recruitment video and a training program. Once you know your company has them, use them. Nothing squelches a business opportunity faster than finding yourself with someone who wants to know more about your business just as you remember you gave your last brochure to your brother-in-law.

7. Products people will want to buy. Your company's products don't need to be proprietary; giant network marketing companies have made billions of dollars by selling laundry detergent and cosmetics. Just make sure the network company you choose offers products people want to buy, either because they are an exceptional value, they're of exceptional quality or because they offer exceptional service and convenience. Whether it's life insurance or air filters or food supplements, your customers must want or already use what you have to offer.

8. Emphasis on products. Legitimate networking companies compensate their distributors for sales, not for sponsoring others. Their compensation plans are based on making sure the company's products get to end customers, whether retail or wholesale. Distributor enrollment fees are reasonable, usually under $50. Legitimate companies do not require a large investment in inventory, known as front-loading. And they offer a liberal buy-back policy for any unsold inventory. In addition, look for a company that offers your customers a money-back guarantee on products they purchase through you.

9. Room to grow. Brand new companies offer plenty of room to grow, but they also offer a greater degree of risk. Carefully evaluate the level of risk you want to assume in your new business. Do not automatically rule out companies who already have a strong market presence. Some very large and very successful companies already have tens of thousands of distributors, yet those who join still find success. There's no denying it may take more time and effort to build a large organization with a company that already has established a substantial presence in an area. That's why some networkers prefer to join a company that still has plenty of room to grow. But remember, in network marketing, you are building your business by introducing your products to those you know. Even if most of the rest of the world already uses your company's products, your friends and family may not and you can still build a business by sharing your products and business success with them.

10. Distributor support. Networking is a simple business, but it's not easy. Those at the top already know what works and what doesn't. There are keys to success in networking, just as there are in any endeavor.

As a beginner, you may not know all the keys yet, but that's okay. Make sure the sponsor and the company you choose are committed to helping you learn them. Strong support from your company's product knowledge department, marketing department and area coordinators can mean the difference between success and disappointment. Strong support from your sponsor, as well as their sponsor and their sponsor's sponsor, are vital to reaching the level of achievement you have chosen. Before you join a company, ask how much help you can expect from those above you in your organization.

11. A product you love. In your career as a networker, nothing will make your life simpler or more enjoyable than a catalog full of products or services you believe in. If you use and enjoy your company's products -- and you must, for success -- you won't be able to keep yourself from recommending them to those you know.

Remember the last time you saw a movie you particularly enjoyed? Chances are the next day at work you recommended it to your co-workers. They may have gone to see the movie on your recommendation and taken a friend or spouse along with them. If they liked it, they may even have recommended it to others, who then also went to see the film. That's how sleepers turn into box office smashes.

Well, what if you received a check from the theater for each person you or your friends sent to the movie? It would be a pleasant extra income, but you would have recommended the movie anyway, because you sincerely thought it provided a good evening's entertainment. Your company's products should play the same role. You want to choose a company whose products you would use even if you did not market them or receive any compensation from their sale. Then your enthusiasm for them will spill over onto other's efforts and benefit everyone involved.

12. A sense of fun. One additional entirely lighthearted piece of advice: find a company that's fun. Find one that inspires you to greater heights of creativity, one that attracts positive and joyful people, the kind you'll look forward to spending time with. Many of the people in your company will become your closest associates and dearest friends. Make sure they add beauty and quality and integrity to your life, as well as income to your pocketbook.

As YOU BEGIN YOUR NEW BUSINESS, you will want the best training you can get to make sure you have the greatest possible chance for success. Imagine that tomorrow when you arrive at your office, your boss calls you in and presents you with an offer like this one:

> "We like what you're doing here. We think
> you have a great future with this company.
> We see a period of strong growth ahead,
> so we've decided to invest in one of our
> most valuable assets -- you.

> "We'd like you to go back to school to
> get that advanced management degree
> you've talked about. We'll pay for the

education. You can schedule your classes
after work and on weekends. It probably
will take you less than two years. When
you've completed your work, we will
immediately raise your salary by $1,500
a month. And you'll have an education
that will benefit you the rest of your career.
All you need to do is invest some of your
spare time. Are you interested?"

Believe it or not, many -- maybe even most -- of those
presented with this opportunity would say no. Change is
difficult and habits, even habits like watching television
every evening, feel familiar and are difficult to break.

Yet when successful network marketers, as entrepreneurs, begin their business, they accept an offer much like
this one, whether they know it or not. They choose to take
some of their free time and invest it in their future. They
make a commitment to study with those more experienced
in their field in order to increase their skills, and they put
what they learn to immediate use in their business.

Students enrolled in a graduate-level course on network marketing would learn the newest approaches to the
basics of the business. They would learn how to duplicate
what they learn so that all others in their group could share
their success and they would practice ways to use their new
skills on the job.

Let's listen in. First, the basics.

THERE IS ONLY ONE SUREFIRE WAY to build a solid networking business. It requires no selling and no persuasion,
and anyone can do it. There are other bells and whistles and
fancy fenders available -- they're next -- but this basic
model will take you anywhere you want to go:

1. Use your company's products and services. Whatever your company makes that you can use, use it. If it is a product, don't wait until you run out of what you have on hand. Using all your company's products sets a good example for those who may join you in the business. You never know when the practice may lead to new business. Imagine one networker's embarrassment when a friend admired her shade of lipstick. If she had been wearing one of her company's lipsticks, she might have won a new customer.

2. Each month, buy the amount of inventory your company requires to remain active. Buy it, as we say in our company, "to use, to share and to show." Use your company's products or services at home, give them as gifts, have them available to prospective customers and build enough inventory to demonstrate products to those you sponsor.

3. Find five people and teach them to do the same. That's all there is to it. Then help your people find and teach *their* people.

THAT'S IT.

As you establish your business, your sponsor will teach you how to most effectively put the fundamentals into practice, as well as the latest techniques to help you build your business in the most efficient way. To speed you on your way, we offer a few additional ideas for rapidly building a vibrant business:

1. Tell your friends, your family and your co-workers about your new business, of course.

2. List everyone you know. Everyone knows several hundred people. Get their names down on paper. You don't need to call them all now, but write down, as many names as you can -- your plumber, your veterinarian, your sister's best friend. As names come to you, whether in the middle of the night or during dinner or while you're watching a movie, jot them down and then add them to your list. Your goal is to make a list of everyone you know by name and then to add to the list as you meet new people.

Review the list often and think about how what you are offering could be of value to the friends you find there. Does someone have dry skin? Perhaps your company offers an effective moisturizer. Is another friend on the list under stress at work? Perhaps one of your nutritional supplements would help provide relief. Would your oil additive protect the engine of your neighbor's new car? Perhaps your weight loss system is just the ticket for the co-worker who mentioned he would like to lose a few pounds.

Perhaps someone on the list is worried about not having enough money or is concerned about losing contact with their teens. A networking business can make a terrific family project, especially when everyone knows the additional income will go toward a joint family goal.

3. Don't prejudge whether someone may be interested in what you have to offer. Even millionaires may be looking for an opportunity that offers a growing income with less effort or stress. Doctors' incomes, as we mentioned earlier, rely solely on their time with patients, and they tend to have to work long stressful hours to pay for their costs of doing business. Many would welcome a part-time business that allows them to multiply their efforts by combining them with others. Stockbrokers, bankers, physicians, artists, captains of industry -- all have built successful networking businesses. In fact, those who are successful in one field often are more able to envision success in another.

Yet don't rule out those who are still struggling to find their place in life. Just as many people who are unemployed, undereducated or hard-pressed have risen to find great success in network marketing.

4. Put your sponsor to work for you. If you decide you would like to grow your business, the best way to do that as a beginner is to find people for your sponsor to talk to. Tell those you know about your new venture, then invite anyone who asks to know more about your products or about the business opportunity to speak with your sponsor:

> "You're right, Alex. I am excited. This is a quality company. And it's a great chance to own my own business. The potential is there for a significant income. But I have to tell you, I'm new at this. I'm still learning the ropes myself.

> "Tell you what, I'm having coffee with my sponsor tomorrow night. Why don't I stop by and pick you up? I'll probably only have about half-an-hour with him, but you'll get a kick out of Tom, and he'll be able to answer some of those questions."

5. Put the printed word to work for you. Send a press release announcing the opening of your business to your local newspaper. Don't forget any specialty business publications in your area. And pass out your business cards. Go through them as fast as you can. Leave them with your tip as you leave a restaurant. Stick them on bulletin boards and include a couple any time you pay a bill.

Some networkers place advertisements in newspapers and trade journals, looking for others who may want to join them in their business. In their training materials, Dayle Maloney and Tom Schreiter both offer excellent guides to using advertising media. We tell you how to obtain them in Appendix A.

6. *Practice a couple of easy ice breakers.* Ice breakers allow you to meet people and give you a natural way to talk about your business. For instance, think of how many times you have waited in line to buy a ticket for a movie. Perhaps it is your habit to strike up a conversation with the person in front of you and chat for a moment about the weather or current events.

During a natural pause in the conversation, it's very easy to pull out a business card, smile warmly and say,

> "You know, you're easy to talk with.
> I'm always looking for people like you
> to work with me in my business. May
> I give you my card? I have no idea if
> you would ever be interested in what
> we're doing, but feel free to give me
> a call about it any time."

Then change the subject. You don't need to mention it again. If they're interested or curious, they'll ask you more, and as you gain experience you will become comfortable talking more directly about your company.

7. *Use video and audio kits.* One of the most exciting developments in networking has taken place in just the last few years, as companies and groups around the country have produced videos or audio tapes that present a company, its products or services and its business opportunity. The use of these video and audio kits can dramatically and quickly multiply your own efforts.

Video kits do two things. They move products and sponsor distributors. A study by the Wharton School of Business showed that video brochures increased retention by almost 50 percent and expedited buying decisions by as much as 72 percent, compared to print advertising. The study also found that three times as many people were likely to request a video as ask for printed information. They were six times more likely to respond to an offer made in a video brochure than to a printed ad.

Video kits can be used both locally and long distance as a screening tool. They can help you find those who want to know more about your products or business. Time is money, and video kits are one way to leverage both.

Typically, a networker builds a number of kits. Each may contain the company video, a brochure or catalog, perhaps a sampling of the product and several business cards. Networkers simply loan out a kit to someone they know, then return in a day or two to pick it up and answer any questions.

Again, let's look at this technique through the doubling concept.

If, as your business grows, you have 10 distributors, each with 10 video kits, that means that at any given time there is the potential for 100 presentations. One hundred distributors with 10 video kits means the potential for 1,000 presentations, each given exactly the same way.

Even if you decide to take a day off, you will know that your representatives, through video kits, are giving professional presentations to hundreds of potential business builders or customers. Video tapes are particularly effective because they never have a bad day; they are never more excited or more complacent one time than another. They tell the story exactly the same way, every time. They present a true ability to duplicate your message with those you contact and they allow you to quickly reach many people.

If you choose to rapidly build your business, experienced networkers recommend you pass out at least one video kit six days a week. Two days after you loan out the first kit, return to pick it up. Answer any questions, and then pass it on to someone else. The next day, pick up the second kit and do the same thing. You will be reaching 12 people a week -- those you gave the videos to last week and those they're going to this week.

One comfortable way to pass out video kits or other information about your company is called a third-party referral system: you ask those you know to refer you to someone else who might be interested in what your company has to offer. When you talk with that person, mention who made the referral. If you were to make contact by telephone, the conversation could go like this:

> "Judy, my name is John Smith. Sandy
> Nelson and I were visiting yesterday and
> she suggested I give you a call. My wife
> and I have just started a new business
> and we're looking for a few sharp
> people to work with us. Sandy mentioned
> you might be what we're looking for.
> I'm curious, are you open to any offers?"

Judy is sure to want to know more! Even if it turns out that she is not interested, she may know someone who is. A variation to the third-party referral offers the chance to obtain even more contacts.

> "Judy, my name is John Smith.
> My wife and I have just started a new
> business. It offers some of the best
> personal care products around, as well
> as the opportunity for a substantial
> second income. Sandy Nelson suggested
> that I call you. She thought you might
> know of someone who is looking for
> what we have to offer."

8. Avoid a hard-sell approach. Each of our suggested business builder ideas relies on an easy and natural way of talking with people. That's important. Hard sell went out of style in the 1980s. Today's consumers and potential distributors are more sophisticated. No one wants to be browbeaten, even with the opportunity of a financial lifetime. Sharp networkers inform people of what they're doing, let them know they would like to do business with them and then keep in touch, lightly. They look for ways to offer value and they let people know they respect their right to make decisions that are right for them at any given time.

THE ONLY ADDITIONAL KEY to any successful network marketing venture is to find what works and repeat it. Repeat it again, and then teach those you sponsor to repeat it. It's a concept known in the business as "being duplicatable."

All efforts in networking are measured by whether they can be easily and correctly duplicated. As author and noted success trainer Tony Robbins teaches, success leaves clues. Just find and emulate someone who has achieved the level of success you desire.

You don't have to figure out network marketing on your own. You can select a company that already is enjoying a high level of success. And you can choose a sponsor within that company with whom to work. It's not like going to work for IBM. In the traditional corporate world, you can't decide which company you want to represent, then walk in, find out who is the nicest boss and request to work only with them. But you can in network marketing. You can select a company and then ask to speak to two or three of its top people. You can interview the leaders and select one to be your personal mentor. If they are the type of leader you're looking for, they will be pleased to work with you.

In addition to working personally with your own mentor, each company contains top groups whose members can offer many valuable insights. And leaders in the network marketing industry itself have authored many excellent guides to success. Some of the best are listed in the back of this book. Your company's training system, combined with those available from these professional network trainers, will quickly get you started on your advanced degree. With them, you have available to you proven methods for success from the first minute you open your business.

CHALLENGES

AND CHOICES

"*Jonathan Livingston Seagull* will never
make it as a paperback."
— James Galton, publisher,
refusing an offer by MacMillan
Company to bid on paperback rights
for Richard Bach's best-selling novel.

Ten years later, paperback sales reached
more than 7 million copies.

I T'S GOING TO HAPPEN, so you may as well plan for it.
It could be your sister, your mother or your best friend,
your racquetball partner or your golf caddy. You're
going to go to someone whose opinion you value, brim-
ming with excitement about your new business. Before
you're even halfway finished describing it, they will look at
you and say, in the same tone of voice they use to discuss
the Internal Revenue Service, "This isn't one of those
pyramid schemes, is it?" And then their mind will snap
shut. You'll be able to hear it clang closed; nothing you will
be able to say will make a difference. It happens to
everyone.

Some people just don't want to hear about network

marketing. Ever. Even if they love you and would ordinarily support you in any way they could. Some people are just suspicious of the unfamiliar. Or maybe they've been hit by one too many hard-sells. Maybe they know someone who has had a bad experience with multi-level marketing. Perhaps they themselves at one time chose a bad company or suffered through a bad sponsor. Either way, they may have ended up with a garage full of products, a credit card full of charges and an address book full of former friends.

Ouch.

Luckily, if you choose to become involved in network marketing, most of those you approach with your new venture will be delighted at your enthusiasm and open to what you have to present. But if you find yourself hurt when someone you care about doesn't seem happy for you, take a deep breath and then take a second look.

They are concerned for you. They may be leery that you're going to pester them to buy things they don't want or to join a company they don't care about.

Even success can be threatening; they may fear you will change and grow away from them. They may even assume that everyone else shares their opinion about network marketing and urge you to drop the idea. All of those things are okay.

Over time, they'll see that although you talk about your work with enthusiasm, you let them decide at what level they want to be involved. They will see that your business adds to your life. It doesn't take you away from them.

"I made it a point early that my close friends and family would almost have to force me to let them buy from me," said one beginning networker. "And now they do."

Sooner or later, those who were skeptical will ask to try a product or two and before you know it, some of those family members will become your biggest boosters.

Until then, believe it or not, no one has to share your enthusiasm for your business. Although it is ideal to have the wholehearted support of your spouse, your family and your friends from the beginning, it's not necessary. Many networking fortunes have been built over others' objections, yet by the time those fortunes were well under way, most doubters had long before climbed on board.

Not every one will want to buy your products, and not every one will want to join your company. But plenty will. Your job is to find the ones that do.

How? By sorting.

PERHAPS ONE OF THE OLDEST network marketing stereotypes is that networkers try to trick people into doing business with them or that they berate friends and family into buying their products.

How unproductive and unprofessional.

Today's networkers stress the word networking. They seek to build long-term business relationships based on respect and integrity. They do business with associates in a way that is mutually beneficial by offering valuable goods and services to a growing and willing marketplace. As they prosper, they are able to offer their business opportunity as an exciting possibility for others. Perhaps more than anything else, they demonstrate that networking is convenient and pleasant.

To find their markets, good networkers sort through people.

They speak openly and joyfully about their company, their products and their business. When appropriate, they offer to share their information and enthusiasm with others. They never try to convince anyone, and they never take rejection personally.

"You never know why someone says no," said one

experienced business builder. "Maybe it's not the right time for them. Maybe they're feeling stressed. Maybe they had a bad breakfast. Just remember, a 'no' doesn't necessarily mean no. It can mean 'maybe later.'

"Rejections happen to all of us. If you're not getting rejections, you're not working your business. When it happens to me, I just make a note of the conversation and move on. They're not saying no to me, they're saying no to this opportunity for right now."

One Seattle salesman agrees, with a witty twist.

His designer auto license plates read, "SWSWSW." Puzzled, we one day got the chance to ask him what the letters meant.

"I'm a salesman," he said. "I sell for a living. And every time I approach my car, those license plates remind me of the saying I have adopted as my words to live by. The letters stand for, 'Some will, some won't, so what!' "

Indeed!

As network marketers build their businesses, some will choose to join. Others won't. So what!

MODERN NETWORK MARKETING CAN OFFER new business owners the training and education they need to make their businesses a success. It also can offer advice that will help newcomers avoid the disappointment and defeat too many earlier networkers experienced. In general, inexperienced network marketers make one common mistake.

Nine out of 10 people who feel they have failed at network marketing believe the company, the product or the concept just doesn't work. They hear about the industry's superstars, the ones who ended their first year in the business with $100,000 of income and a stable of silver BMWs. After a few weeks or months, when they don't see the same results in their own business, too many get discouraged and quit.

Hear us, now.

There are only two basic elements to success in networking -- dedication and persistence. People who fail at network marketing stumble for only one reason: they quit too soon.

"I can't tell you how many times I've seen someone quit just before things started to happen in their group," said Marlee Huber, a networking professional with several years of experience. When that happens, success doesn't bypass your group. It just bypasses you.

Think for a moment about a new attorney setting up a first practice. Would you counsel that attorney to consider the beginning of that business from the day he or she accepted the first case or from the day they entered law school? Probably you would suggest that they count the beginning of their business from the day they actually began to practice law, after completion of their education.

Yet new networkers too often start counting how long they have been in business from the day they sign on with a company, even if they have no prior experience in network marketing. They are too hard on themselves; they allow no time for education. Then, if their new business doesn't yield a significant profit immediately, they get discouraged. They end up looking for the rewards of an advanced degree when they're only halfway through the program.

Remember our fictitious friends, Andy and Samantha? At the end of their first year in networking, they had few distributors in their network, little sales volume and no business builders in sight. But they continued their work.

One year later, they were working with Samantha's Uncle Mike and a growing group in Detroit. Before long, they had been joined by Andy's sister's friend, Janet, who quickly developed her own group. Within three years, their struggling little venture had evolved into a prosperous and growing business enterprise.

Tom Schreiter, a top national networker known for his series of "Big Al" training books, tells a similar story. Tom and his wife became networkers early, when Tom was in his early 20s. Without the training tools available to networkers today, they managed to make about every mistake possible. After almost two years, they had no distributors, no sales volume and few prospects for the future. But that didn't stop them.

"We didn't know we could quit," Tom said, laughing at his own story. "Our sponsor didn't tell us we had the option to quit." He and his wife continued to work at their business and today Tom Schreiter is one of networking's superstars. He has reached his goals and fulfilled his dreams, all because he didn't give up.

As a beginning network marketer, you will do a lot of things that you do not immediately get paid for. But as your business grows, there will come a day when you will be paid for a lot of things you do not do. That's what makes network marketing different from working for someone else. When you have a job, you exchange your time for your employer's money. In network marketing, you exchange time up front for a substantial income later.

SUCCESS

LEAVES CLUES

_____

"Whether you think you can
or you think you can't, you're right."
— Henry Ford

MEET DAYLE MALONEY, Jan Ruhe and Tom Schreiter. Maloney, Ruhe and Schreiter have built large network marketing businesses, but they may best be known for how skillfully they pass along to others what they have learned. Their commitment is to teach others how to achieve as they have. If success does leave clues, these three have many of the answers.

DAYLE MALONEY:

"I knew when I got involved in multi-level marketing that it takes time to build a business," said networking legend Dayle Maloney. "Still, I kept hoping against hope that the checks were going to come fast."

Dayle had watched the network marketing industry for several years before he took the concept seriously, only dabbling a little here and there. "I think I'd been enrolled in 20 different companies and never done a thing in any of them," he said. "Never did get a check. But I was always intrigued by the power of duplication."

Then, in 1983, while presenting a series of business seminars on the West Coast, he took a second look. The story of just how the Maloneys finally began a network business is an entertaining one.

"I got involved in March," Dayle said, recalling the beginning. "In that one month, I sponsored 164 people on my front line. Now, *anybody* knows you can't work with 164 people, but I didn't know any better. I was just putting them in every day, all month long.

"Well, my first check was due April 25th. I really knew these people hadn't been going very long. Most of them hadn't even received their sales manual yet. They hadn't bought any product, but still I kept thinking maybe the check will be halfway decent."

On the day his first check was due, the future networking superstar walked out to the mailbox. "Here was an envelope from the company," he said, continuing his story. "*Awfully skinny...* It was a long walk back to the house. I opened up the envelope and the check there looking at me -- my first check -- was for $5.66. I told my wife, 'I quit.'

"Well, it's funny. About two days after I quit, a good friend called me and said, 'Hey, I've got a hot deal for you.' What do you suppose it was? The same company. I said, 'That's no hot deal.' "

Dayle really had quit. In the next month, he referred at least 25 people on to his friend. Then one month later, he received a second check in the mail.

"I opened up the envelope and the check was for a little over $527," he said. "Some of those people had started to work. Well, I got interested, but I still wanted to see what would happen. The third check really caught my attention. The third check was for $2,640. I told my wife, 'Hey, I'm going back to work again.' "

He did. In 1986, Dayle Maloney's gross earnings from

network marketing reached $200,000. By 1990, they had reached $459,000, and Dayle estimates his 1992 earnings, thanks in large part to the 30,000 people in his downline organization, will reach $800,000.

Today, Dayle and Jeannine Maloney are network marketing leaders. In addition to building one of the largest businesses in the industry, Dayle Maloney has gone on to help others achieve success through his seminars and training programs.

"I guess that's what that $5.66 check taught me," he said. "You have to have patience and stickability in multi-level marketing."

We've told the story of how Dayle, as a young high school graduate, was struck with polio just as he was preparing to leave for the University of Wisconsin, where he planned to turn his love of sports into the physical education degree he needed to become a sports coach.

"I wanted to get well above everything," he said. "I took extra treatments, forced myself to move my weakened muscles."

Even from his hospital bed, he shaped his future in his own individual way. As his condition improved, his friends would come to the hospital, load him into a car and take him to a Dairy Queen for his favorite treat, a chocolate malt. "I set a goal then that when I got out, I would see what it took to get a Dairy Queen store," he said. A few months later, family and friends helped him raise the $17,500 he needed to buy a Dairy Queen franchise. At age 19, Dayle Maloney became the youngest operator of a Dairy Queen.

In the years that followed, Dayle became a reporter, then a businessman and sales trainer. By 1983, he was ready to take a second look at network marketing.

"Dayle Maloney is the epitome of those leaders who make things happen," writes Dayle's friend Robert Natiuk, in their book, *They Dared To Be Free*. "For three decades he set sales records across the nation, using his unique blend of Wisconsin simplicity and his unstoppable enthusiasm."

Dayle and Jeannine Maloney have helped people across the U.S. improve their lives by teaching them to build second-income businesses. His motto: "If you continue to think like you've always thought, you'll continue to get what you've always got. *Is it enough?*"

JAN RUHE:

Her children were young when Jan Ruhe, then a Dallas homemaker, attended a Discovery Toys party in 1979.

"I fell in love with the product line the first time I saw the toys at a toy party," she says in her autobiography, *Pour Yourself a Cup of Ambition.* "I said to myself, 'I will be buying children presents for Christmas and birthdays for the next 15 years. I should get into the toy business. I'll be meeting new mothers, and it will be fun for the children to play with the toys...' "

Jan started her business with a $300 gift from her grandmother, two babies under the age of three and another one on the way. She turned a spare bedroom into a demonstration playroom and installed a telephone line.

"Most of the time the meetings were held in my home," she said. "We put up Port-a-Cribs and playpens in the bedrooms. We did whatever we had to do to get the job done."

Her early days were often hectic and frustrating, yet in 1980, her first full year in business, Jan was named Discovery Toys' top manager. She has been at the top of her company ever since. Unfortunately, other types of challenges loomed. In 1985, at the end an unhappy marriage, Jan entered into a painful and expensive two-year battle for custody of her children. Through it all, she was determined to grow as a business owner and as a person.

"I was listening to tapes by all kinds of speakers, went to many seminars, read thousands of pages on motivation and personal growth," she said, recalling that difficult time. "I read biographies and autobiographies about champions... I now realize that only when someone is hungry for information will they go hunting for it."

Jan first sought out those with the survival skills she needed and then began to share her own expertise with others. In 1988, she produced a motivational audio tape set, *Don't Be Average; Be a Champion* and began her Champion Network seminars.

"I could not afford *not* to be self-motivated," she said. "I had a responsibility to myself, my team and my family. I started to think success. I listened, researched, probed and evaluated. I realized that I was the one to make the final decisions about my business and my life. I did not hesitate to be a pioneer. I began to take risks and make mistakes. I let success, not failure, rub off on me."

Today, Jan Ruhe travels the world with her children and new husband. She earns more than $200,000 a year. She has sponsored more than 500 people into Discovery Toys careers and her downline includes 5,000 "dynamic, wonderful, excited people."

"The rewards I have achieved in MLM are many," she said. "MLM lets me have the flexibility to work the hours I can and take off when I need to.

"MLM has changed women's rights. Everyone who joins MLM has the same opportunity, whether you are a man or a woman, whether you have college training or not or support from others.

"There are enough people who have become successful in MLM who are willing to show others the light on the trail. Break all those past limits. Someone is always winning. It might as well be you."

TOM SCHREITER:

Deep in Texas legend lives one of network marketing's greatest teachers, Big Al.

Big Al always knows just what to do. Fumble a presentation or botch an opportunity and Big Al will come through to set things right. Big Al may seem to be larger than life, but he really lives in Tom Schreiter's imagination. Tom's series of Big Al books have taught quality network marketing to thousands of today's networkers. Big Al may always know the answers, but he learned them from Tom Schreiter.

Tom has been using his dry sense of humor to teach success principles since the first Big Al book was published in 1985. "I've been basically an introvert, to be quite honest with you," he said. "I'm a pretty quiet, low-key type of guy."

Tom has authored four Big Al books so far. More will follow.

"We wrote the first one because we made all these mistakes," he said in the voice of Big Al's straight man. "Then we made some more mistakes and wrote the second one. We made some more mistakes and wrote the third one; made a *lot* of mistakes and wrote the fourth one. Now we're about three books ahead on mistakes. All we basically do is list our mistakes so people can say, 'Yeah, I did that too,' or maybe, 'I can avoid that one.' "

Originally, Tom wrote his books primarily for his downline. So far, they've sold more than 200,000 copies in countries across the world. The books have introduced many people to network marketing, but they also are one way Tom builds leaders in his own network business.

"I have a firm belief that multi-level marketing is just building leaders and making them successful," he said. "It means a long-term investment in people. It's not a get-rich-quick thing, yet there's an opportunity to do quite well."

Tom was born on a Nebraska farm. He joined his first network marketing company early, in 1972 at age 23. "I got married," he said. "And like most married couples, we needed extra income. I could either work a part-time job until I was 65 to make ends meet or I could have a part-time business in MLM. It was the only business I could afford. Back then, it cost $18.75 to get started and we financed that."

The Schreiters saw an ad in the paper, went to an opportunity meeting and liked what they saw.

"For the first year and 10 months, we probably were the hardest working couple you ever saw," he said. "We went to every opportunity meeting, every training meeting, every seminar, every company function. We went to a lot of retail presentations and at the end of one year and 10 months, we basically had no customers and no distributors. So the first year and 10 months were a little bit slow. It took a while before we got our first break."

Yet they never thought of quitting.

"We didn't know we could quit," Tom said. "We didn't have any downline to quit, so we didn't know it was possible. Our sponsor never told us we could quit. We just assumed that was it. Hooked forever. But being naive paid off. After a year and 10 months, we got our first break."

Almost two years after they had started their business, the Schreiters sponsored their first business builder. "That got us some customers and a little momentum to get started," Tom said.

The slow start didn't discourage them, Tom said. The Schreiters had made the decision that first night that network marketing was to be their future.

"It's just that we had no skills or any idea how to do it," he said. "Back then, there was no one to provide training. No books, no general training courses." Instead, they learned the old-fashioned way, with plenty of trials and more than a few errors.

"Once, I recruited a guy during jury duty," Tom said. "He came to an opportunity meeting and brought a woman, about age 46, who had 12 children. Her husband was disabled. They lived on $432 a month of government aid.

"The bottom line is, that man dropped out a few months later, but the woman went on to become a superstar, making $20,000, $30,000, $40,000 a year, getting trips and cars. And I ended up making about $1,500 a month on bonuses because I hung in there. Her sponsor dropped out for a $700 a month job."

Tom bases his training on practical, easy-to-duplicate principles that provide a clear picture of what network marketing has to offer. He presents it all with a grin and with a realistic idea of what it will take to make it to the top.

He doesn't promise quick or easy riches.

"What I think works most effectively is to talk about a person who is making $3,000 a month and who makes $1,000 a month part-time on top of that," he said. "In that $3,000 budget, a person may have $100 left over for themselves. By adding $1,000 a month, you've taken that 10 times further."

The additional income can make the difference between financial discomfort and prosperity. "You could throw that $1,000 into the bank and be a millionaire in 20 years," Tom said. "Or you could take a vacation for two to Cancun once a month. There are so many things you can do with $1,000 a month extra. A regular job takes care of all other needs, and this is free money."

Tom looks for potential leaders, for those who are willing to invest effort into their business and into themselves. "The secret to MLM is to build leaders and make them successful," he said. "I look for people who want to be a leader. They may not have the skills yet, but that's okay."

That's when Big Al begins his education process. Tom's advice:

"Scratch out the first six months or a year" to learn the business, be your own best customer, use all your company's products and then, as you learn your business, teach others.

"You're going to invest a lot of time (with those you sponsor)," he said. "You're going to be a mentor. It's as if I move in with my prospective leaders for five or six months. We'll be doing two-on-one presentations together as they get on-the-job training. And they see they're going to be doing the same thing with *their* leaders to get *them* trained."

At the end of six months, those who make a solid commitment to network marketing should be able to make a good presentation and should be working with several potential leaders of their own, Tom said. At the end of their first year, they could have "a couple of very good leaders and $1,000 a month in extra income," as well as a good start on a secure future.

As he talks with people, Tom looks for those who already are attracted to network marketing.

"I like to find somebody who *wants* to work the business rather than try to force them to," he said. "While other people spend a lot of time convincing people, I look for someone who doesn't need convincing. They understand it is a business they're going to build, versus a lottery in which they're going to talk to three people and get rich."

Network marketing has allowed Tom to reach his goals -- and to create Big Al. "It's a great industry," he said. "To be quite honest with you, I've gotten a lot more out of it than I've put in."

9

A

BEGINNING

"It is one of the most beautiful compensations of this life
that no man can sincerely try to help another
without helping himself."
— Ralph Waldo Emerson

*The children ran ahead as Tom and Susan Edison stepped
off their jetway and began to climb the brick path toward their
house. It was good to be home.*

*One of the best parts of their business was the chance it gave
them to travel the world, visiting associates who long ago had
become friends. But another was the opportunity to return, as
always, here to their home. After a couple of weeks away, a glass
home in the middle of a high Colorado meadow seemed just the
place to be.*

*"Andy and Samantha looked good, didn't they?" Susan
asked Tom, unconsciously reaching out for his hand as they
walked. "I think she's right. Her new group is going to take off.
Looks like the next few months will be busy ones for her and for
me."*

*"You've taught her well," Tom said. "And her top level
people are fireballs. You'll probably be able to handle most of
your end from here, don't you think?"*

"Yes. I don't plan to stir for the entire winter. There are too

many things I want to do here. Like gaze into a fire."

Tom laughed. "I've heard that before," he said. "Remember what you used to say when you were first starting the business? 'I can inch my way to the top where I am or I can fly to the top on my own.' You've really taken flight, Sue."

Susan squeezed his hand and laughed. "You thought I was crazy," she said. "It took you two years to admit I hadn't taken leave of every single one of my senses. Remember my first bonus check? Not quite $4."

She paused. "Where do you suppose we would have ended up if we hadn't become networkers?" she asked.

"Wherever it would have been, it would have been okay," Tom said, as they reached their deck. "We would have made sure of that. I'm just glad we made the choices we did when we did. Come on, do you want to order a movie or screen the new product holograms. David said he'd have them here this evening."

"You go ahead," Susan said, sinking into a chair beside the pool. "I'm going to sit here for a few minutes and watch the sun set."

Dusk gathered as Susan leaned back in her chair and thought back to their trip and to the friends they had visited. Tomorrow would be a busy day...

As the meadow darkened, the lights inside the house began to cast brighter reflections into the hydropool until they seemed to pull her inside to her family.

"Look back?" she said to herself as she got up and turned to the house. "No. Not ever."

T HE DISTANCE BETWEEN OURSELVES and our futuristic friend, Susan Edison, may not be that great. One networking company already is using satellite technology to revolutionize the way it communicates with its distributors and with those who want to learn more about the company and its products.

Cellular Nutrition, a one-year-old division of Herbalife, uses interactive conference calls to make presentations to thousands of people at one time. Those who attend a conference -- one of more than two hundred a year -- are called *at home* at a predetermined time. From their home in any of a number of countries, they join others to listen to a master of ceremonies talk with people around that country about their experience with Cellular Nutrition. Those who choose to join the program have the option to receive training from the company's top leaders -- and to build their own business -- primarily by interactive conference calls.

The program, designed by Herbalife's Mark Hughes, Lawrence Thompson and Larry Huff, allows distributors to build a worldwide organization as easily as one in their own community.

We believe Cellular Nutrition's high-technology approach to business is a herald of the communication and business revolution that lies ahead.

Technology already is cutting new frontiers through the way we live our lives, until it seems that our futures are racing toward us at the speed of light. Even though we sometimes feel we are whirling in a confusion of change, we know the decisions we make today will shape all else that is to come.

Like those early in the century who watched with awe the approach of Halley's Comet, we all can choose to view the future with apprehension or, with knowledge and an open mind, with anticipation. That is our choice.

When a brand new century finds Susan Edison on her Colorado mountaintop, we believe those who today choose network marketing also will find themselves looking out over their own vistas of opportunity and accomplishment. That too will have been their future choice.

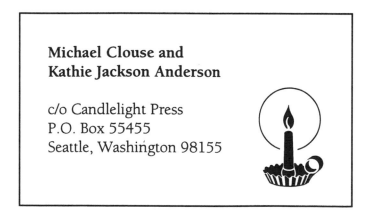

A S YOU MAKE THE CHOICES that shape your future, our thoughts and good wishes go with you. We invite you to learn more about network marketing and about how your own networking business can help you build the life you desire. We've listed a number of excellent resources in the back of this book and how to obtain them.

And please, contact us as well. If we don't know the answers to your questions, we'll help you find them. That's how network marketing works. Neighbor to neighbor, new friend to new friend.

**Michael Clouse and
Kathie Jackson Anderson**

c/o Candlelight Press
P.O. Box 55455
Seattle, Washington 98155

BOOKS:

Materials marked with an asterisk (*) are available from Candlelight Press. For complete ordering information, send a stamped, self-addressed envelope to:

Candlelight Press
P.O. Box 55455
Seattle, Washington 98155

* Failla, Don *How To Build a Large, Successful Multi-Level Marketing Organization, Advanced Edition*, Multi-Level Marketing International, Inc., 1984.

Hutton, Shirley *Pay Yourself What You're Worth*, Bantam Books, 1988.

* Kalench, John *The Greatest Opportunity In The History Of The World*, 1991.

Natiuk, Robert *Your Destiny: Your Life and Your Work Become One*, 1991.

Natiuk, Robert and Maloney, Dayle *They Dared to be Free,* Success Unlimited Publishers, 1986.

* Ruhe, Jan *Pour Yourself a Cup of Ambition,* 1992.

* Schreiter, Tom *Big Al's How To Build MLM Leaders for Fun and Profit,* Kaas Publishing, 1991.

* Schreiter, Tom *Big Al's How To Create a Recruiting Explosion,* Kaas Publishing, 1986.

* Schreiter, Tom *Big Al Tells All,* Kaas Publishing, 1985.

* Stewart, David *Network Marketing: Action Guide for Success,* Success In Action, 1991.

* Vinberg, Emil and Dean, Athena *Network Marketing Today,* 1992.

VIDEOS AND TRAINING SETS:

Gage, Randy *How to Earn $100,000 a Year in Network Marketing,* Gage Research and Development Institute, 1992.

* Maloney, Dayle *Secrets of Multi-Level Marketing, Vol. I & II,* Dayle Maloney & Associates, 1989.

*Millionaires In Motion *Network Marketing: Your Magic Carpet to Personal & Financial Freedom,* 1992.

Nightingale, Earl *The Strangest Secret,* Nightingale Conant.

*Paradigm Communications *Network Marketing: A Special Investigative Report,* 1991.

Success In Action *Network Marketing In Action*, 1991.

BOOKS ON BUSINESS TRENDS:

Aburdene, Patricia and Naisbitt, John *Megatrends for Women*, Villard Books, 1992.

Branson, Robert M. Ph.D. *Coping with the Fast Track Blues: A Survival Guide for your Climb to the Top*, Doubleday, 1989.

Celente, Gerald *Trend Tracking*, John Wiley & Sons, 1990.

Clason, George S. *The Richest Man in Babylon*, Bantam Books.

Clifton, Donald O. and Nelson, Paula *Soar With Your Strengths*, Delacorte Press, 1992.

Edwards, Paul and Sarah *Getting Business To Come To You*, Jeremy P. Tarcher, 1991.

Edwards, Paul and Sarah *Making It On Your Own*, Jeremy P. Tarcher, 1991.

Eisenson, Marc *The Banker's Secret*, Villard Books, 1990.

Gross, Andrea *Shifting Gears: Planning a New Strategy for Midlife*, Crown Publishers, 1991.

Hallowell, Edward M., M.D. and Grace, William J. Jr., *What Are You Worth?*, Weidenfeld & Nicolson, 1989.

Holland, Philip *How to Start a Business Without Quitting Your Job*, Ten Speed Press, 1992.

Popcorn, Faith *The Popcorn Report*, Doubleday, 1991.

Whitlock, Charles R. *How To Get Rich,* Contemporary Books, 1991.

APPENDIX B:

OVERCOME THE

NO-TIME SYNDROME

Millions of networkers are building a successful part-time business in their spare time. How often have you heard, "I'd like to, but I just don't have the time"? There are 168 hours in every single week. Where does the time go? Take a look:

Activity	Time Spent	Time remaining in the week
Sleep: 8 hours/day	56 hours/week	112 hours
Full time job: 8 hours/day	40 hours/week	72 hours
Commuting: 2 hours/day	10 hours/week	62 hours
Eating: 2 hours/day	14 hours/week	48 hours

Activity	Time Spent	Time remaining in the week
Family & entertainment: 2 hours/day	14 hours/week	34 hours
Miscellaneous: 2 hours/day	14 hours/week	20 hours

According to a recent A.C. Nielsen survey, the average American watches 49 hours of television per week. How much is the TV habit costing you? $5,000 a year? $10,000 a year? More? Kicking the TV habit could make you rich.

"I gave up television," said Eunice Vinberg, a top network marketer. "I decided I could watch Dynasty now or live it later."

ETHICS

SIX WAYS TO GAUGE A COMPANY'S INTEGRITY

1. Today's quality network marketing companies *offer legitimate goods and services at fair prices.* The company's primary goal is to get its products to the end user, the wholesale or retail consumer.

2. *Compensation is based on sales, not recruitment.* Distributors earn commissions and bonuses based on the amount of sales, either individual or in their group. Payments are not made for recruiting alone.

3. *Sale of goods and services must be the company's primary focus, not the growth of its distribution network.*

4. Legitimate network companies *do not require distributors to buy large amounts of inventory with which to begin a business.* And they offer liberal buy-back policies in the event a distributor chooses to leave the business.

5. *Unreasonable claims about the amount of income possible from network marketing are prohibited.* Although the rewards to a successful marketer can be staggering, those in the

company and its networks are diligent in fairly presenting income opportunities. Network marketing is not a get-rich-quick scheme. As any business venture, it rewards those who are willing to work hard and who display persistence and creativity.

6. The top network marketing companies *belong to some type of industry organization* such as the Direct Selling Association or the Multi-Level Marketing International Association, whose members subscribe to a code of ethics that is monitored and enforced.

The DSA, MLMIA, the Federal Trade Commission, state attorneys general and other consumer groups offer additional information on how to judge network marketing and other business opportunities.

Kathie Jackson Anderson is a West Coast business editor and award-winning reporter. She writes for a number of nationwide publications, primarily on matters of business and personal finance. She is a fellow at the Knight Center for Specialized Journalism at the University of Maryland and a member of Investigative Reporters and Editors, a society of investigative journalists.

A beginning networker, Anderson discovered the industry while researching a story on entrepreneurs. She and her youngest daughter live near Seattle in a delightful 95-year-old house they are trying, somewhat successfully, to renovate.

From a door-to-door salesperson at the age of 19 to an executive with a multi-billion dollar international corporation just 10 years later, **Michael S. Clouse** has been teaching, motivating and helping people reach their greatest potential for almost a decade. His students have included employees of some of America's top companies, including AT&T, Nynex, Toshiba America Corp., and Packard Bell Electronics.

A lifelong student of success, he has trained with the nation's top success leaders. Clouse began his network marketing career in the mid-1980s and today heads one of his company's fastest growing groups.

When he is not teaching others, one of his favorite hobbies is horseback riding -- but only on Tuesdays, when the weather is fine and there is no rain. He and his family live in Seattle.

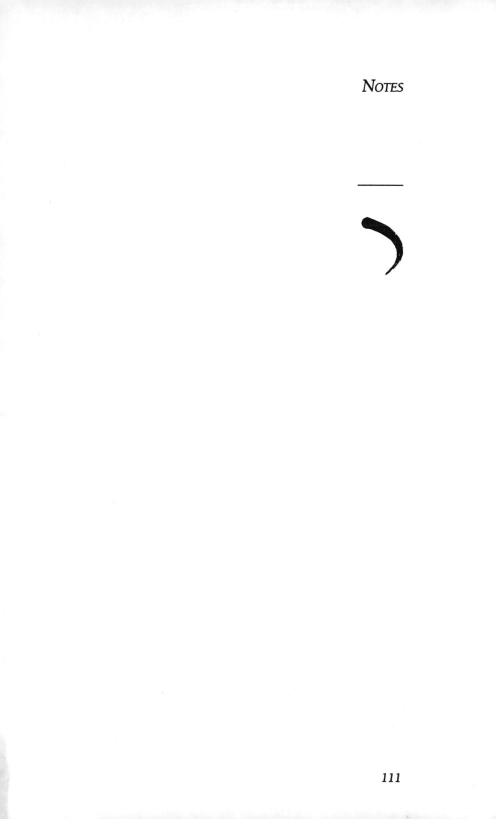

Future Choice was designed and typeset by Emily Silver.
The type is ITC Berkeley Oldstyle.
Candlelight Press Logo concept & design by Taylor Clouse.

Special thanks to: June Bigelow, Ashley Clouse, September Clouse, Scott DeGarmo, Cary Falk, Bev Habib, Miles and Kathleen Jackson, Larry Levy, Lynn and Darryl Kuntz, Dayle Maloney, Alexandra Nixon, Brooke Nixon, Jill Nixon, Rob Nixon, Jill Rouw, Jan Ruhe, Tom Schreiter, John Sestina, and Kelly Thayer.